MW01248468

"A deep meditatio experience, Alec B. minder of memories, and a love letter to emotions we lose ourselves in. A mixture of love, loss, madness, and the existential thoughts that grip us, Hood explores the meaning of death and how it follows us on both positive and negative fronts."

— Flor Ana, Author of *The Truth About Love*

"With *Rest in Pretend*, Hood invites us into a surrealist dream, perhaps the fragments of a soldier's life flashing before them as they bleed out on some battlefield on a remote continent of the world. The poems run on into each other, with no clear division between them, a stream of consciousness that seeks to understand the nature of morality, if there is a reason that justifies violence, and if love can truly redeem."

— Renzo Del Castillo, Author of *Still*

"*Rest in Pretend* explores the intricacies of grief and introspection with eloquence and delicate respect. Dressing darkness almost as a gentle hero, Hood fearlessly reflects on the bitterness and eventual medicine that comes from sitting down with our demons. Each poem in this collection offers readers a cathartic contemplation of the profundity that is the human condition. The layered metaphors translate the nuances of layered emotion encountered when one experiences and works through unsettling trials and confining tribulations that can break the spirit. "

— Elizabeth Knightly, Author of *Choose To Choose Me*

"Hood weaves a melancholy web of loss, grief, and heartbreak—with love finding its way through the cracks. The illustrations bring an added dialogue to the poetry that is sure to tug at the feelings that bury themselves within us all."

— Fin Rose Aborizk, Author of *On the Ever-Lovely Morrow*

"Hood's grief is raw and sometimes painful to see, but he takes you with him through his allegories to a place where anyone can relate. You may shed a few tears, but you will definitely marvel at his sensitivity and intellect. *Rest in Pretend* is not seeking answers, it is not offering answers; it is grasping your arm and pulling you down to the precipice to peer at the depths. This vulnerability is sublime"

— Erin Flanagan, Author of *Haikus to Irish Tunes*

Cover Art Copyright © 2024 by Chris B. Murray
Illustrations Copyright © 2024 by Anouk de Vries

Edited by Flor Ana Mireles

1st Edition | 01
Paperback ISBN: 979-8-9906352-1-0

First Published June 2024

For inquiries and bulk orders, please email:
indieearthbooks@gmail.com

Printed in the United States of America   1 2 3 4 5 6 7 8 9

Indie Earth Publishing Inc.
| Miami, FL |

www.indieearthbooks.com

INDIE EARTH
PUBLISHING

Rest in Pretend

(poems)

Alec B. Hood

Illustrated by Anouk de Vries

Those who I would dedicate this book to are
no longer here to read it, but even so, I am certain that
all the emotions mixed into this medley of ink and paper were
either entrusted to their ears or buried with them.

"He in his madness prays for storms,
and dreams that storms will bring him peace."

- Mikhail Lermontov

Rest in Pretend

i pride myself in existential conversation
but we can just talk about the weather instead

and i promise not to ask you
why you wear long sleeves in july

we can just look for our favorite animals
in the canvas of clouds above

i don't really know how to cook well
but it's hard to mess up grilled cheese

so if you'd like to stay for lunch
i promise not to ask you

about the missing kitchen knife
that's in your sock drawer upstairs

but if you ever want to be heard
i am not going anywhere

and i hope
neither are you

and who knows
you may find out

that i am pretending
just as much as you

i took the muse's bargain
and turned my shadow into an endless inkwell

i couldn't understand my own sorrows
but through poetry i could at least give them names

and so i made a maze out of metaphors
and purposefully got lost in it

and at the time it was just a dream
but now it's pretty clear

i was never a poet
just a prisoner to poetry

and my pursuit of the pretend
was simply just a refusal of reality

but i could still tell you love stories
and leave out the tragedies that ended them

and i could still lift your spirits
and be the bygone left below

i could still be somebody you love
and somebody you don't know

my muse marveling from within the ink
so beautiful and yet so grotesque

i can no longer tell if it is saving me
or if it is the source of my self-destruction

is my shadow a cemetery
where both my soles and sentences sink   . . .

or is my shadow a blanket
where both my windpipe and words obtain their warmth

i am marching
in time's rearview mirror

and i am wondering
if i will still be on my feet

when time is at its adventure's end
i don't know and so

today i will make a memory
kind enough to grow old and die with me

maybe i'll plant a vegetable
and smile when it gets rained on

or maybe i'll try mustard for the first time
even though i already decided i don't like it

or maybe i could wear a cape
and learn to dance the jitterbug with my wife

or maybe i could befriend a cow
name her meryl and feed her dandelions

or perhaps i could just forgive myself
and dislodge this sword sewn into my soul

but i don't know and so
i am marching

and i am wondering
if i were to be left behind

would my love linger in a lonesome limbo
or make it to the finish line without me

i can still hear his mother on the phone
asking if her son is dead

i told her the doctors aren't sure what he took
but they're trying their very best

she stayed on the line and wept quietly
until her son and i left the hospital together

but he couldn't look at me anymore
and my words weren't reaching him

i knew he needed the kind of help
that we weren't equipped to give

and that eventually led to his apartment floor
where the world left his eyes

i never spoke to his mother again
but i know he was buried 3,000 miles away from her

maybe his corpse would only bring questions
instead of closure

her son the soldier
who was sent overseas

her son the veteran
who couldn't afford a headstone for himself

but none of this is his story
because that lies in the little things he laughed about

or in the dreams he secretly chased
or in the kind memories he'd cling to when scared   . . .

those are the things that matter
and the things he never shared with me

*The Veterans Crisis Line is a United States-based crisis hotline
for military veterans, service members, their families, and caregivers.*

If you or a loved one need help, dial 988.

my first cicada season
i was almost ten

i remember enjoying their company
and their constant chorus in the canopies

i often held one in my palm
and petted the veins in its wings

but with so many broods buzzing about
many children came to the conclusion

that they could kill them without consequence
and better yet impress their peers while doing it

one kid dribbled a ball between his legs
flattening the insect in the process

another kid managed to drown one
in the cafeteria water fountain

and when all their eyes gazed upon me
i just wanted to somehow hide in my bedroom

but their taunts tangled with my trepidation
and i sacrificed my sensitivity for their approval

i plucked the cicada out of my palm
and placed it between my molars

when its wings vibrated against my gums
i instinctively gritted my teeth

and the kids i aimed to be embraced by
were now scared of me   . . .

and instead of a pal in my palm
i had guts glittering in my gullet

and because of that
i was more alone than before

i remember the raccoon
trapped within that trash bin

clawing against the sides
stuck and squeaking

it scared me so i ran for help
and my father came and freed it

but he told me i saved its life
and that made me feel good

that's when i understood something
that so many seem to grow up and forget

that if something feels pain
we probably shouldn't kill it

and that if something has parents
then it will be missed if it does not return home

i remember wanting to grow up
so i wouldn't need to ask for help anymore

and i remember thinking as the raccoon ran
that it probably wanted to grow up too

when i allowed myself to grieve
i didn't do it right

and because their hearts were quiet
i believed i couldn't break them

but i can see them now
and in their eyes the gentle truth

that not even heaven
could stop me from hurting them

so if this is to be
the last poem i ever write

then it is simply
an apology to paradise

it felt impossible to be positive
when my audience were already ghosts

but even in my failures
and especially in my self-hate

they loved me anyway
and that was enough

why do they sing to me
the skeletons on the seafloor

why do they swim to the surface
and share their stories

they become the ghosts
that fill my room with life

the nightmares
that i insist i don't deserve

and with such gentle violence
they remove the top of my skull

they peel back my dura matter
and play the piano on my brain

and it's an ugly sound
but they still sing to it

and when they hit the final note
i wonder what happens to me

and i wonder what happens to them
do they ferry me to my fate

or do they become a stowaway
in someone else's dream

i counted the bullet holes in his body
like how a mother counts the freckles on her firstborn

i counted until i lost count
and wondered if it was worth starting at zero again

but then an image floated to the forefront of his pupils—
a memory that had left his halted heart in a hurry

there he was wearing a bedsheet as a cape
a child wanting to be a superhero

"bad guys can switch sides if spared"
he lectured his mother while she laughed

"that's why you capture instead of kill"
he persisted as his mother pretended to listen

the child didn't know
that he'd grow up to be a bad guy

and he didn't think
that the heroes would not spare him

but as that memory evaporated with his future
i wish that they had

that sad shimmer that swims upstream in space
it is the last breath of a stubborn star

it is so desperate for an audience
to acknowledge its audacity

and so it gallops across the galaxy
dead set on becoming a corpse on your curb

self-delivered and signed for
with no return address

but to us stars are just strangers
whose bodies dissolve in the light

and the only evidence they ever lived
is the sight of them dying every night

they took my grandpa out of the sixth grade
so that he could be his mother's caretaker

and he never went back to school
and he probably never understood

how the woman who raised him so sweetly
could succumb to an invisible sickness

her mind rotted long before the rest of her
and nobody told him it wasn't his fault

and so instead of making friends at school
he made excuses for his mother's meanness

and then she started to tear apart his flesh
despite having once put it together

but he endured her disease until its death
praying over a closed casket with open wounds

and then he left without ever looking back
with only an elementary school education

the factory work served as salvation
until he maimed his hand in the machinery

and every family has a villain
but i didn't want mine to be my grandpa ben

but the monsters he met when only eleven
would be introduced to his own children

all his forlorn feelings fell through his fingertips
and landed on his kids like blows from a belt   . . .

but neither his story nor the scar tissue on his soul
could provide an adequate excuse

and perhaps he understood that
but i can't speak for the dead

still i hope my grandpa is forgiven
even if only forgiven out of mercy

but i imagine wherever he is
he is happier now

because his children
broke a cycle that he couldn't

i only became a vampire
to have an excuse to wear a cape

plus i figured that whenever i felt bloodthirsty
i could just simply bite my lip

but then people got hurt
and i played a part in it

and soon hurting myself
couldn't quench the craving

and so while the sun still slept
i dug up the dead

sunk my teeth into their despair
and drank it like blood

but it was only when the children caught me
and encouraged the carnage

that i felt sick to my stomach
and so i spat at their feet

reminding them that one day
the sun would steer them towards salvation

but for me all it could ever do
is sear my skin to cinders

maybe in the distant future
let's say a few hundred years from now

a mad scientist will be moved
by the magnitude of our love

and the stillness of our skeletons
will stir a sadness in her stare

and it's not enough for her to perform our poetry
in the presence of our apparitions

and so she organizes new organs
around our old memories

and it allows us to exit heaven
and sin together again

and we will dance above
our own overgrown gravesites

and laugh at the soil
that once sunk its teeth into us

and we will make bouquets
out of what bloomed from our bodies

and put on papier mâché masks
made from our obituaries

but perhaps most importantly
now that our patchworked parts won't perish

we can leave love notes
handwritten on each other's hearts   . . .

and our love will never be on the menu again
no matter how loud death's stomach growls

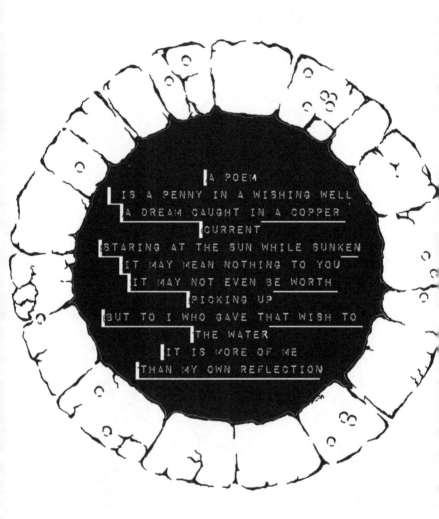

A POEM
IS A PENNY IN A WISHING WELL
A DREAM CAUGHT IN A COPPER
CURRENT
STARING AT THE SUN WHILE SUNKEN
IT MAY MEAN NOTHING TO YOU
IT MAY NOT EVEN BE WORTH
PICKING UP
BUT TO I WHO GAVE THAT WISH TO
THE WATER
IT IS MORE OF ME
THAN MY OWN REFLECTION

we figured the farm fed his family
while we crushed his crops

the farmer's tears gave it away
but his face remained expressionless

the route ahead scared us
and so we turned our vehicles around

it wasn't personal
but it was enough to destroy his livelihood

later we found some roadkill that had thumbs
and it shared that same expressionless face

blown up and bisected
by the bomb he had buried

everybody laughed at him
the debris of a desperate father

but if we could subpoena his soul
and project his point of view

then the contours of our courage
may lose their shape

and so sandwiched between
the planet's core and crust

the farmer's story
has long since been buried in the sand

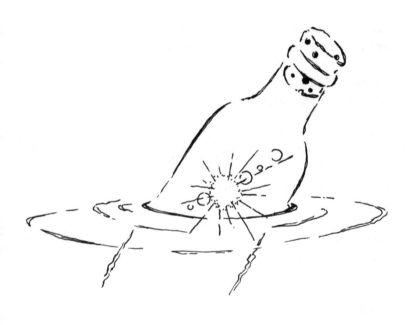

her grief evolved from a feeling
into more of a frenzied flaying

the unfastening of the very fabric
found beneath her flesh

it caused the compass in her cranium
to lose its calibration

and so she fired a flare gun
far off for the heavens

and with it the hope that its light
wouldn't be hidden by the sun

but as her soul soured into sepsis
that solar shine swallowed her distress call

she always told me she thought of a prayer
as a message in a bottle

a wish wandering the waves
swimming towards shores with winged skeletons

and in her death rattle she sung out
to that ocean of unanswered prayers

causing it to spill into the solar system
and drown the stars she once wished upon

from there it sunk the skies
and not long after, extinguished the sun

in the seventh grade i couldn't stomach the liquor
and so the older kids offered me pills instead

and they squeezed my pupils to a pulp
so i couldn't see the joke

i didn't understand why i was laughed at
but i understood that i was angry

and i felt so empowered by that rage
and soon so emboldened by bullying others

and because i couldn't trust myself
i found a uniform that kept me out of trouble

and i racked up a debt with the government
as an incentive to stay alive long enough to settle it

and because i lived such a pathetic story
out of pity i was given the keys to pretend

where i could use such beautiful words
which are way easier to love

than me

sometimes there is no sequel
and no silver-lining

only an unrevised reality
that hovers overhead

just like this quiet man
suspended in the air

trying to take his body
with him to heaven

is there anything profound in this?
any catalyst for change?

retell the story
review the facts

a man went into his garage
and never came out

but he wore a winter hat and gloves
while he waited to be found

and there it is
the relief that rushes in

because now we know
that he wasn't cold when it ended

and that has to be enough
because that's all there is

the gentle poet woke up underwater
neither wet nor with breath
drowned in this purple sea

the man sunk with no signs
of self-defense or survival instinct
he sunk until he floated
and he floated until he free-fell

the impressive emptiness overwhelmed him
he never figured the absence of everything
could have such an overflowing presence

the violet hue that surrounded him
soon became his favorite color
or perhaps just the only color he could remember

soon he questioned if his eyes still worked
and soon after that
he questioned if he still had eyes at all

but then he saw the jellyfish
their heads like oversized umbrellas
lighting up his surroundings
with a baby blue glow
that burst through the beautiful nothing

this allowed the gentle poet
to see the white whale
covered in scars
left by the last-ditch efforts of other men

and once the whale opened
its welcoming mouth
and revealed all it had swallowed   . . .

the gentle poet had all of his answers
the most evident being
that somehow he had died

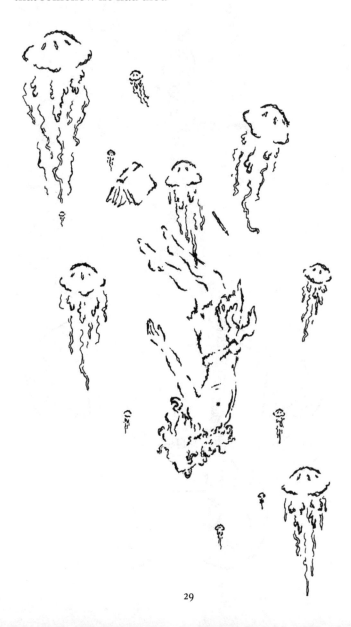

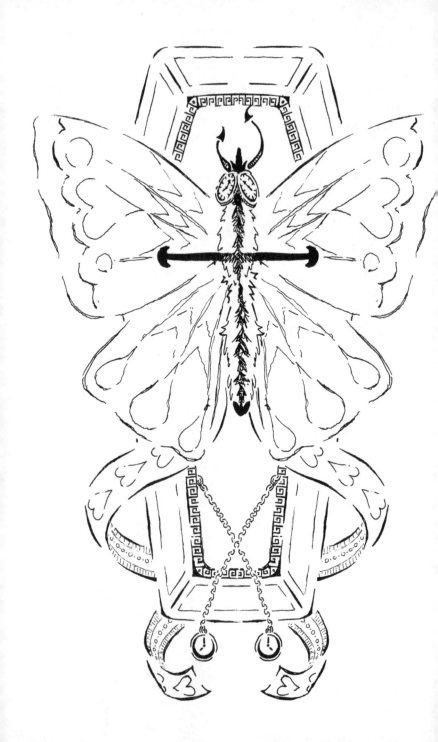

mourning has its own magnetic field
and in that maze it is easy to get misdirected

that's how i ended up in the past
packing my pockets full of memories

and wading into those waters
where "what could have been"

is reflected in the riptides
like doorways to our most desired dreams

i thought time further separated us
and so i yearned to never leave yesterday

until i saw that blue butterfly
that i hadn't seen since one landed on your casket

and when it flew towards the future
my feet were too frozen to follow

and it made me wonder
if i had it all wrong

what if every day brought me closer to you
instead of farther away

that would make time a unifying force
and with it the wisdom

that moving forward
could never mean leaving you behind

i followed the lightening bugs to be here
with the hopes of saying something profound

but the only thing i have to say
is that i think i'd be happier

if my wife allowed me
to put a lava lamp on my bedside table

and then i could watch the wax shapeshift
into things like cactus-flavored candies

or into those dinosaurs
whose heads look like battering rams

or even into a circus of cicadas
that use their shells as surfboards

i think what makes lava lamps so lovely
is that they're like minds encased in aquariums

it's as if our imagination melted out of our ears
into a liquid gore that glows in the dark

and then put into a jar
and plugged into the wall

yes i'm certain of it now
that would make me happy

the child noticed a ladybug
stuck in a spider's bed

the poor girl danced in horror
as if dying to a rhythm

so the child freed her
and he felt good about it

his heroics had him
rethinking the value of life

and for the first time he wondered
if bugs had hearts

but before he got his answer
he saw the spider

and subsequently squashed it

LOVE IS AN ARMOR CARVED FROM DIAMOND
DURABLE AND DETERMINED
WE WEAR THESE CRYSTALS TO BED

LOVE IS A LIFE-RAFT HURLED INTO ANDROMEDA
AUDACIOUS AND AMBITIOUS
WE ANCHOR EACH OTHER IN ZERO GRAVITY

LOVE IS A SIMPLE STORY
EACH BREATH A SENTENCE SANG TO THE SUNRISE
AND SO BY NIGHTFALL

WE ARE NOVELISTS

if you had made it to fifth period
you would have failed your math quiz

and your mother would've lectured you
about the importance of math

while doing your math homework for you

if you had made it to fifth period
you would have made eliza laugh

and you would've noticed her dimples
and wondered about her favorite things

but really you'd just want her to laugh again

if you had made it to fifth period
you would have been teased

you would've rushed to be there early
and having done so forgotten to zip up your fly

beet red you would've waited for the teacher to intervene

but you never made it to fifth period
because you're still on the cafeteria floor

you only understood death
in the context of great grandparents and goldfish

you had never heard a gunshot before

well it's his anniversary
and the poor custodian is working overtime

mopping up
all the schoolchildren's blood

his wife is waiting at the restaurant table
and the waiter feels so awful seeing her alone

and so he refills her glass of red wine free of charge
but she'd secretly rather just pay for a gin and tonic

at the school the custodian slips on some brass
and twists his ankle really bad

and so he limps out of the crime scene
and into a sea of candlelight

the veterans on the street complain
about how the flag is always half-staff

while the senators shine their lapel pins
and shrug their shoulders

at the restaurant his wife looks over the bill
but before she can sign it

the custodian rips it up
and gives her a kiss

he orders her a gin and tonic
and she is so happy

that she doesn't ask about his limp
or the bloody boot prints that he leaves behind

should we slam the book shut
and save ourselves from their stories?

a professional pianist
diagnosed with parkinson's disease

he still practices every day
but he will never play again

a woman with stage four cancer
working the drive-thru

saving as much as she can
to see a beach before she dies

a woman six months pregnant
and only six weeks sober

narcan chasing opioids
through her placenta

a teenage girl left overdosed
on the floor of a running shower

the scans show no brain activity again
and so the family asks for a third hospital's opinion

maybe to come any closer
would be to close in on calamity

but as these pages pile up
so do the lives lost on the library shelf

but perhaps the angels are avid readers
and so these stories will find their way above   . . .

and these faces carefully not forgotten
will somehow witness heaven

even if it is only just a glimpse
reflected in god's reading glasses

it was the greatest rhyme i ever wrote
and it was the best night of my life

i remember the alphabet against my skin
its letters falling to my feet

until the right words just stuck
like dried blood on a blade

it was a beautiful rhyme when i went to bed
but by morning it had become ugly

and that's when i knew
that i'd never be a poet

and what made it worse
i knew i'd never stop trying

if a pound of flesh
is worth an ounce of soul

then why does the source of her self-worth
center solely on her skin

and why does it seem like every other step
she hovers above society's scale

this woman at the meat-market
consumed by every environment she enters

self-hatred isn't something she has
but rather something she was taught

by the everyday surroundings
that stood to profit off her insecurity

and i can see her eyes avert
every time she passes a mirror

and now she's searching for self-love
in the side effects of these pills

but it isn't her fault
that we convinced her she wasn't beautiful

this design is deliberate
we sowed the seeds of doubt into her smile

we told her that she wasn't enough as is
and unfortunately for her

she believed us

sharing my mind
with embalmed bodies

has only ever gotten me here
alive on the autopsy table

holding my breath
in anticipation of the first cut

i don't have the courage
to tell them i'm not a corpse

besides i have this awful feeling
that i am exactly where i should be

and so the buzzsaw
sings to my skull

reminding me of the ceiling fan
in my childhood bedroom

such a gentle white noise
that always puts me to sleep

it is always a bad idea
drinking with taxidermy

the deer's head hung on the wall
with tears welling up in his glass eyes

i tell him that he has my sympathy
but that it won't change anything

and that upsets the deer even more
and so i cowardly turn my head

i order another ginger-ale and vodka
but only because they are out of ginger beer

you know if my poetry could save a life
or could make it so getting killed didn't hurt

then i could have been of use
and i wouldn't have had to ignore that deer

but if i am to be both haunted
by my own helplessness

and looked down upon
by the helpless that hang above me

then perhaps i have misjudged my situation
and it is in fact the deer who pities me

after all it is obvious
which one of us deserves heaven less

and so i escape into the sunless streets
because i have no desire to discover   . . .

how ugly i must look
from behind the deer's glass eyes

i sat down in the shower
until it became a sauna
at the site of a subdued sun

and suddenly the curtain
turned to the wing of a bird
and the ceiling swung open

the lemonade rain poured in
twice the lemon juice and sugar
too sweet for everyone else

my favorite stories
are written in the writhing roots
that swim to the surface to be read

and the dragonflies buzz
to the beat of the bird's song
keeping the beasts asleep

and the sunflowers are so tall
that i can't even see the flower
but the stem is beautiful enough

i have been to this place once before
it's called the cherry blossom boulevard
and it is where i learned to smile

a symphony speeding down the streets
a chorus coming from the cows

but with no instruments or voice
they bang their heads against the wall

they know where they're going
and so they know there is no tomorrow

and so faced with such despair
they make music

maybe it is to get god's attention
or maybe it is just to annoy the driver

but nonetheless they find a song
somewhere in begging for their lives

but when the answer is no
and the melody dies with them

in the blood-soaked silence
all that remains is a poem

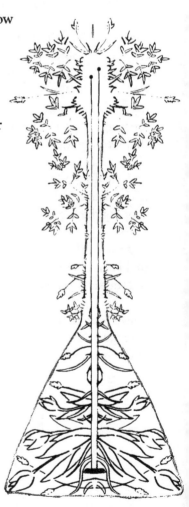

my earliest memories of you
are ones where you're afraid

afraid that god would read your poetry
and think that what you wrote was stupid

you always took it personally
when god didn't answer your prayers

as if it were somehow your fault
as if you were somehow easy to forget

and so you wanted more than anything
to impress god with your words

and i wanted more than anything
for your story to not be a sad one

but it was foolish of me
to dismiss your desperation

just like it was foolish of you
to ever think god would call your poems stupid

still you promised to keep writing
and run your favorite rhymes by me

but after vacation bible school that summer
i never heard from you again

there was once an angel whose wings
were comprised of countless quill pens

she jumped off the high dive in heaven
and left that sanctuary for good

and with each aerial maneuver
she authored odes to the atmosphere

and soon she scribbled sonnets in the sky
baptizing our planet in poetry as she plunged

and once submerged in the saltwater
she recited limericks to the sea life

her work is in every wrinkle in this world
and she walks within our wildest wonders

her oldest poems are carved into tree trunks
which have long since outlived our ancestors

and those ballads in the bark suggest
that when god found her on an autopsy table

she had no interest in peace or paradise
and so she resolved to rest in pretend

where the alphabet became her urn
allowing her ashes access to every imagination

where they stir the sparks of the stories
that are sleeping deep within our souls

perhaps the best parts of me
are buried with my brother

and these words aren't poetry
but rather an inventory of all i've lost

the electricity in my eyes
and the liveliness in my love

the self-esteem in my steps
and the belonging in my breath

somehow i have become
an echo in search of its origin

the exhale of a ghost
that eclipses the candlelight

but even in the most perfect dark
his smile is as easily seen as the sunrise

and its warmth is like an ember in my vein
that thaws my hypothermic heart

so perhaps the best parts of my brother
are not buried with him

and these words aren't a surrender
but rather a promise to find him again

i woke up nineteen years old again
with my parents by my bedside in tears

but instead of breaking my bathroom mirror
this time i just went back to bed

whatever they have to say to me
they've already said it before

and whatever wounds await me
the blood is already in the sink

and whatever words i write next
the end result is already written

and so i purposely misplace my pen
so i can instead feel my pulse

and pretend that it belongs to him
and that it'll still be there in the morning

séances and stories
shaped my oldest friend

and to quench his creativity
he manufactured midnight monsters

and mistook their mouths
for morning miracles

and when his wounds smiled
they drooled blood

leaving him knee-deep
in death's saliva

where a simple misstep
or sudden memory

means a slip n' slide
down hell's esophagus

and when sitting within that stomach
the imagination is the first to melt

and so i begged him
to never write again

because it is a thin line
between a dead poet

and a poet
that is obsessed with death

he was addicted to the pain
long before the pills

he lived with a second shadow
that always seemed to overstep

i watched him lie through absent eyes
every sentence straying from sincerity

and soon his story stopped
and i hadn't stuck around to see the blood

some people liken themselves
to candles in the dark

but that was never him
in fact if anything

he was the darkness
that kept the candles company

and nothing i write could ever change the truth
that when he needed help the most

i wasn't there

when someone dies
something of them ought to survive

because we never stop waiting
for them to come home

we are patient for their return
until we realize it is us that must go to them

and that's the coldness of life
our great tragedy

we must go to heaven
whereas hell can come to us

that hell can hold us hostage
in our own bodies and homes

and somehow i have found myself
shackled to my own silhouette

a prisoner to pandemonium's poet laureate
pinned to the partition of his panopticon

but even so to hurry to heaven
would be to leave a poem unfinished

and when someone dies
something of them ought to survive

and most times
that something is us

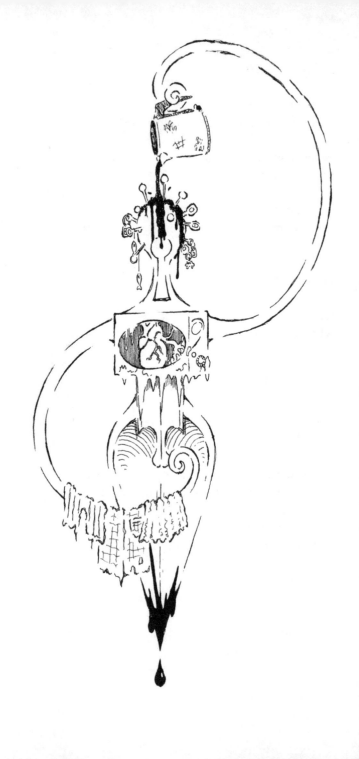

when i misplaced my car keys
you asked me where i saw them last

well it was last wednesday in the kitchen
when i handed you that scorching cleaver

so that you could fish out my frozen heart
and put it in the microwave

we watched it dance in circles
beneath that center spotlight

the rare red baked to a gray brown
and i told you it was a job well done

and you told me you loved me
but i was already dead on the floor

but as my body bent backwards
i saw the keys behind the coffeemaker

so i should start searching there
and then check the pockets of what's in my laundry

i celebrate you with the birds
even though you are afraid of them

and i celebrate with our sweetheart dog
and all the squirrels that are afraid of her

i celebrate with the creatures that come and go
with the raccoons in the trash and with the cat on the porch

and even with the possum in the backyard
that i couldn't bring myself to kill

i celebrate with the soil
and everything that sunk into it

with all the souls and fossils
tangled up in the tree roots

i celebrate with love poetry
because it is read by both heaven and earth

and perhaps if i piled up pages to paradise
or wrote rhymes in a liquid rose gold

then my love for you could be hugged by hardcovers
and entrusted into eternity's library

but at last i celebrate with you my wife
i have got you both presents and pie

but maybe you'll just want a bedtime story
the coordinates for a dream we can drift off to together

i knew a man like that

his salvation on his shoulders
the abyss at his knees
halfway to heaven, halfway to hell
eyes mesmerized by a distant desire

that man died on his feet
unclaimed by both above and below
still a servant to an empty throne
the dream that never came true

i remember calling that man a fool
but liking him nonetheless

our skeletons waltz in purgatory
wondering "where is the sun?"

wondering how we bled out
from wounds that we could not see

wondering what is next
and what was before

but if it is true that our smiles aren't ugly
and that we are worth the life left in our lungs

then it is time to gather up our displaced particles
and pilgrimage back to our planet

i have spent an eternity in motion
and it has been a wonderful dance

so wonderful that i have never regretted
losing sight of the sun with you

he picked up the mouse with his hands
careful not to crush her

she appeared kind and curious
like a child in over her head

but she whimpered in fear
upon being raised in the air

and it hurt the man's ears
so he took her to the refrigerator

and fed her a piece of cheese
and pet her softly as she ate

she let her guard down
the way we do when with friends

that's when he sat her down
next to the rat poison

and the man trembled
as the mouse continued to feed

she stopped chewing mid-bite
her dead eyes still grateful to the man

he immediately missed how she moved
now knowing that she'd never move again

it was of no fault of her own
it's just that her life was inconvenient by design

and so the man did not ask for her forgiveness
for he had no need for it   . . .

because someday it will be him
in the gentle hand of a friend

maybe at the mercy of a god or a general
another impersonal affair ending in death

but in a different world
or perhaps a better world

she would finish her meal in peace
and being alive wouldn't be reason enough to kill her

we wanted to share our lifespans
with our dogs

but we couldn't
and so to lift our spirits

we laid in bed together
and watched videos of otters

surfing downstream in shoddy sailboats
never allowing their lover to sink

even holding each other's hands
so that sleep never separates them

and suddenly it surprises me to see
that we're now in the water

wrapped in a raft of seaweed
sharing the sunset with the otters

and i feel inspired to say
that even if the sky split

and a meteor shower struck the surface
spreading tsunamis across the country

i would squeeze your hand harder
never allowing you to sink

sailing off with the otters
into a world with nothing left

falling in love with you
each night again and again

i fell in love over dinner
she ordered the filet mignon
and me the mac n cheese
and i mistook the salt
on the rim of her margarita
for sugar and spit it into my sleeve
and that night for the first time
the stars struck me as ugly
and even unwelcoming
and i was happy to be on earth
even with the terrible things here
like worms in graveyards
and leeches in swimming pools
because she was here
and her warmth
tipped the scales in ways
that not even the cosmos
costumed as the heavens could

i went adrift in my writing chair
and entered the orbit of heaven

where i circled salvation
but never got any closer

and while suspended i saw my entire life
stuffed into the scribbles within my desk drawer

the doomsday poetry
the roadkill obituaries

and a few love songs
that i never got the chance to sing

and so it is not all ugly
even if the ugliness is what persists

but for so long i swore
that if i sifted through the guts and goo

then i could find a deeper meaning
or at best the answer to why

but the truth wasn't in what was left behind
but rather in who still remained

and so i returned to my chair
but instead of writing

i sat next to my wife
and softly sung to her

i can always tell
when reality runs away

because the ceiling fan
turns to waving octopus arms

and the roadside skeletons
stand back up in the rearview

and the acorns tip the hats on their heads
bowing with their brains exposed

and all the faces i failed to save
thank me for saving them

and heaven becomes so heavy
that it implodes from above

and shooting star confetti falls
crushing me to a sticky dust

and then reality returns
and with it—a resurrection

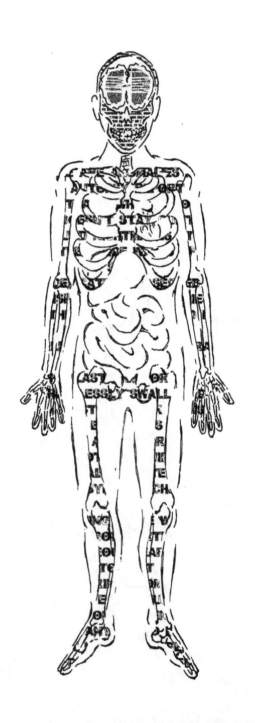

there are anomalies in his autopsy report
and that's why his corpse doesn't stay quiet

we found nightmares stapled to the inside walls of his skull
all delicately dissected and displayed like trophies

and there are memorized bible verses
still embedded in his brain blood

his last cry for help helplessly swallowed
and still stuck in his esophagus

his guts are engorged with both his guilt
and his half-digested dreams

his goodbyes ricochet in his bones
as if begging to be written in rigor mortis

and his hideous heart refuses to halt
still hollering from inside the crematorium

it is horrible enough
for anyone to hope

that upon their death
a poet doesn't find their body

my footing fell apart
when i somehow triggered that trapdoor

and since i have been plummeting
down paradise's sewage pipes

with stormwater settled in my lungs
swirling into cyclones within my skin

but it isn't homing in on hell that hurts
it's getting farther from heaven

and whatever kept me from it
i didn't have the courage to confront

and so i stop clawing my excuses
onto the walls that watch me fall

i could pretend that i was only ever the prey
and that my pulse never felt performative

i could put it all in a beautifully bound book
but i bet god doesn't read melodramatic poetry anymore

and so i won't protest my punishment
and it's purposeless to put me in purgatory

because whatever new path i'm put on
i'll just make the same mistakes again

the footprints on the floor
and the water stains on the ceiling

the belly that kicks
and the artery that narrows

the birth water in the bathtub
and the bloodstains on the street

the first sip of alcohol
and the last gulp of water

the empty crib in the corner
and the do-not-resuscitate orders on the fridge

they are all the same
poems waiting to be written

forever curious
if their story is worth telling

I HEAR VOICES
I'M SURE YOU DO TOO

BUT THE DIFFERENCE BETWEEN US
IS THAT I SOUGHT OUT THEIR SOURCE
AND FOUND MY ANSWER

I WAS RIGHT
IT IS THE VOICE OF AN ANGEL

ALBEIT ONLY A RECORDING
SPILLING OUT OF THE VOICE BOX
OF A CORPSE

THAT'S WHEN I LEARNED
SADNESS IS JUST AS MUCH A SOUND
AS IT IS A FEELING

he couldn't fight the fog
that fed on his feelings

and that's why he isn't here
to tell his own story

he described this fog to me
as a breathing anger

a dancing despair
that smiled at what was missing in him

he said the fog formed into the wrong pieces
and somehow still squeezed to fit the puzzle

and that it painted a peculiar picture
one he couldn't look away from

this picture captivated him
until the fog fell from his eyelids

and exuded from his ears
and soon it was all he could exhale

the fog scraped its way to the surface
so that it could bring that picture to life

and then it dissipated
leaving only its masterpiece behind

there are no hippos in my local zoo
because of a boy and his beach ball

he threw it into the habitat
and the hippo mistook it for a watermelon

and because of that
the hippo never grew up

but twenty-two years later that same boy
stepped into a different hippo habitat

some say guilt guided him there
others say madness mauled his mind

maybe the hippo that haunted him
hauled him there for his reckoning

but a lot can happen in twenty-two years
and so we'll never truly understand it

but this boy found himself so sleepy
that he laid his head on a hippo's tongue

and he saw salvation in its gentle jaws
and so he waited for the gift of the guillotine

he hung his head within that behemoth
and the hippo mistook it for a watermelon

and because of that
the boy never grew old

when i met you at the ferris wheel
you said it spins like a severed head somersaulting

i asked you why you said that
and you answered because it made you happy

and so we sat down for lunch
and you told me about your ex-husband

and the sadder your story got
the wider your smile became

and then out of your lunchbox came the ribs
with a barbecue sauce slightly too red

you removed the flesh with your teeth
and then polished the white bone with your spit

i asked you how it tasted
and you asked if i had ever accidentally bit my lip

we both laughed
until you suddenly snapped the rib in two

you then placed the pieces in my palm
and subsequently said

"imagine being born from something so brittle
when the soil is so strong"

and that's when i saw a sadness in your eyes
sharp enough to pierce through paradise

and an anger in your heart
hot enough to herald in a new hell   . . .

and when i went to get a lemonade shakeup
you were gone when i got back

and that was the first and last time
i ever met a woman named lilith

when i feel courageous
i turn the lights off and shower on

and i sit beneath the water and wait
for all my illnesses to appear

dressed in cyanotic skin that can't be saved
wearing masks made from dismembered memories

they tear themselves apart
and watch me suffer

it's like a police lineup
of silhouettes in the steam

and every poem is an attempt
to unmask the root of the infection

to close in on the source of their strength
by seeing what's beyond the veil

because if i could just see their foul faces
then maybe i'd know how to fight back

i haven't seen my imaginary friend
since he sharpened that scalpel

and used rather poor technique
to cut out my imagination

but there is still a madwoman in my attic
who writes better poetry than me

but that isn't the reason
i fell in love with her

you know sometimes i reach for a pencil
just to find a prescription in my hand

but i'd rather have a pharmacy under my flesh
than the poison that my mind mass produces

do you think i don't know
how unhinged i sound

maybe it is my imaginary friend's fault
because he does not have steady hands

or maybe that madwoman is actually a witch
and i mistook her sinister spells for sweet sonnets

either way my love hasn't been lost to the lunacy
it persists through all this unpleasantness

masked in metaphors
or encrypted in code

my love will always be right here
waiting for you to find it

the little boy pronounced chocolate
like "talk a lot" when begging for it

he reached out his muddy hands
and i had none to give

but even if i did
it was discouraged to appease the children

but i found myself faint-hearted
and so i asked my mom to send candy from home

and when it arrived i packed my pockets full
knowing i'd just allow the boy to swipe it

but the village was different upon our return
and so i sent my translator to investigate

i learned the little boy accompanied his father
to a place he shouldn't have been

and in the dark air above
the boy mistook a drone for a shooting star

and if he wished for heaven
his wish came true

but he probably wished for chocolate
because i can still hear him begging for it

"talk a lot"
trembling from a tiny tongue

and so when a fellow soldier asked me
for a piece of candy from my pocket   . . .

i said no
i'd rather just let it melt

i have no interest in the prayers
of the people that we pretend to be

wasn't it our desire
that descended us to this dancefloor

and wasn't it our love story
that allowed us to lose our minds

tomorrow we may be wilted flowers
but we're beautiful today

so will you find where i have fallen
and forgive the sins on my flesh

i have no interest in paradise
or the promises that it pretends to keep

i want to feel alive in your arms
even if it costs me my life

and when you arrive dressed in embers
walking barefoot on magma

you could baptize me with your embrace
and burn the burdens from my body

and then we could dance away the despair
until we arrive at my demise

but instead of food for flames
i'll be your renegade love

resurrected in a rowboat full of roses
ready for another round   . . .

of this underworld romance

i imagine each poem
is a knock at heaven's door

and so i keep the angels up
so they don't forget about me

because in the company of corpses
the conversation can become uncomfortable

which causes bruises on my broken heart
that my twisted thoughts use as target practice

but no matter how dark it gets
i make sure my eyes never adjust

because all those i have lost
i have found again

not by looking skyward
where the sun swallows my view

but by befriending the shadows
that are still standing in the sunlight

i found them not in the catacombs
but in the community

and not on the epitaphs
but in the tales of their tender hearts

and most of all i found them
in the kindness they continue to inspire

i hatched out of a past life
with no memory of my own

but as if out of ancient instinct
i wrote your name in pomegranate juice

and upon reading it for the first time again
i understood that my love had outlived my life

and so i asked the stage manager
how many times has your name rescued me

and how many exhales from empty lungs
and how many times have we already had this conversation

but before my curiosity could be quelled
a smile subdued my stoic stare

because how blessed am i
that everything can be taken from me

except your name
that i can still feel humming in my bones

and so know that when i am not with you
it just means that i am on my way

and if i should die again
my body can be easily identified

i am the one with "margaret"
carved into his soul

and everything i've done in this life
i've done it while in love with you

i find it hard to imagine
anyone more dramatic than me

ever since i was in the second grade
and that bird broke her neck on my bedside window

it ruined my eighth birthday
but i still left a piece of chocolate cake by her grave

i never learned to throw a baseball
but i could play handball in the neighbor's front yard

there was a rocking chair by their window
but it had been still ever since my neighbor got cancer

people have asked me if i am crazy
but i have never asked myself

except for the time i asked for my wisdom teeth back
so i could put them on a necklace

i showed a pastor my poetry once
and he said he would pray for me

but i never understood why
because this is the happiest i've ever been

i understand that your son is behind this door
but once we force the lock

not only will the latch shatter
but also the illusion that he's still alive

so think hard these next few moments
hold onto hope like you used to hold his hand

and remember what the air tasted like
when you two both still shared it

i'm driving home now
and i swear i can still hear your screams

and to make things worse
i found a half-eaten rabbit in my backyard

and so i scooped it up with a shovel
and turned towards the trash bin

but upon seeing its sad eyes still open
i felt compelled to bury it instead

and the deeper into the earth i dug
the quieter your screams became

until there was silence
and that's when i realized

i never got the chance
to tell you how sorry i am

my friend has this memory
that doesn't belong to him

he tells me of a stowaway nephilim
hidden aboard noah's arc

whose children drowned
and he didn't understand why

and so in his despair
he collects molted angel feathers

and sharpens them into needles
so that any essence of heaven that remains

he can push into his veins
and see his children again

and then he tells me the memory ends
and he wonders if he's seeing his ancestor

and i tell him i hope not
because that means he never had a chance

there was a naked man on the park bench
feeding crumbs to crows

i saw him from a nearby oak
while writing what would become this poem

he continuously clawed for more crumbs
from what seemed to be a bottomless bag

until he looked down at an empty palm
"all gone?" i asked from afar

the strange man just laughed
"not quite yet," he smiled

he then retrieved all sorts of seasoning
and applied it sloppily to his skin

and as the murder formed into a halo overhead
the man stood up for his last words

"it is better to be the one who is eaten
rather than the one who eats"

the beaks blitzed through both his brain and brawn
turning his body to a buffet

i then approached the bench
and sat next to what was left of his now-red skeleton

i saw his skull somehow still smiling
"even if that were true," i replied

"what impact could such an idea have
if it is only shared by the dead?"

it is always these poems
that interrupt my lobotomy

like they are the last words
from a ruined mind

and so before the operation is continued
please write down what i say next

"i am a knight forever kneeling
at the corpse of a king i couldn't save

immune to joy
and incompatible with heaven

with a life that will only extend as far
as my promises to dead men will allow

but still i take the centipedes outside
because my death is the only one i'm indifferent to

and if i am to be just short of salvation
then that means there's an opening in paradise for them

besides it's never been something i deserve
so it's okay that it escaped my reach in the end

i suppose the gate was just too narrow
and the wound was just too deep"

that is all for now
please continue with the incision

there seems to be a misunderstanding
and i hope it isn't my fault

but you don't need anyone's permission
to be beautiful

mine least of all
besides i have been biased

ever since i saw you
with the phoenix nest in your hair bun

leaving those snake eggs
at the entrance to medusa's grave

yes ever since that moment
i have been at your mercy

so whether it be marriage
or make-believe

you are your own majesty
and the moon is the jewel in your crown

regardless i have become a believer
because a beauty that can bewitch even the poets

proves that i wasn't misguided
to believe that you could exist outside a myth

some children use their bandages as blankets
and shiver as the sun slips out of sight

other children are tucked in with the rubble
and they remain still in the sunlight

it is always the skin that doesn't look like mine
that is deemed disposable

and it is always in places where people who don't look like me live
where indiscriminate weapons are unleashed

and if it won't stop with children
then it will stop at nothing

but this is how it has always been
the greatest poets and painters

the most profound prophets and politicians
all buried by us before becoming of age

and now while we're waiting
for hell to hold us accountable

we hope that our pardons and pinned medals
will be honored posthumously

and that god doesn't force us to look
at their limp limbs and lifeless eyes

and ask us the simple question
"do you think this was part of my plan for them?"

i never met a deer
that i thought deserved to die

when i was a kid
a man told me a story

about a mother deer
that moved me greatly

the mother
was traveling with her baby fawn

when she was suddenly shot
right through the belly

and in a split second
she decided to take off

leaving her baby
so she could lure the hunter away

to run with such a wound
it must've been excruciating

but what hurt the mother the most
more than the dangling guts

was that she didn't have time
to look over her baby one last time

her blood trail went for well over a mile
before she became too weak to stand

but even then she tried to crawl
anything to widen the gap for her baby

. . .

the story goes that the mother's mad dash
even caught heaven's attention

and so when the hunter sunk his knife into her
god made sure she didn't feel a thing

"if only humans could be so noble"
the man would finish his story with

and that's why i mourn
what's rotted on the road

because to me every deer i see
is that baby the mother died for

i don't know what heaven looks like
but i imagine it is a place

where my favorite ice cream
is not a seasonal flavor

a place where i have a pet goose
and angels ask if they're allowed to pet it

a place where i plug my heart into the wall at night
so it's easier to get out of the bed in the morning

i wonder if god would take a walk with me
through the moments in which i nearly met him

and i could ask him how to look cool
without putting cigarettes out in my palm

but more importantly i'd apologize
for all that i have wrote

and if he should forgive me
then he should know

that i am not at peace
and the worst is yet to come

before she could float off
towards that faraway kingdom

her husband had hoped to intervene
and so he climbed a nearby building

and jumped from the roof
desperately stretching out his arms

so that he could snatch her ankles
and weigh her back down

but in his attempt to keep his wife on earth
he ultimately fell to his death

now the story would have ended here
had the husband's brother not been a fisherman

but since he was
he cast his line into the river of styx

and with his broken heart as bait
he hoped to catch his brother's soul

and to his surprise
he did

he used every muscle he knew how to
in his valiant attempt to reel his brother in

but the river refused to release him
and the brother refused to let go of the fishing pole

and so in his helpless struggle
he was tugged into the tide   . . .

i tell you all this
not to ruin your day

but rather to simply explain
that when swimming deep towards despair

the real issue at hand
is not the descent nor the destination

but having enough air
to reach the surface again

i'm sure there is a world somewhere out there
in which i never wrote a single poem

because instead i studied our sister species
by playing tic-tac-toe against chimpanzees

and because i won every match
they cut the funding to my research

and so i returned to my hometown
both a failure and a fool

and i locked myself in my childhood room
until i forgot what my own laugh sounded like

that's when the ink first called to me
with pretend promises from lying lips

placing a poem in my blood to balloon
like an embolism buried in my brain

and so to sweat it out of my system
i ran along that rugged road

and in passing the cemetery
i saw that your stone wasn't there

and so because you are still alive
i never picked up the pen

and words were never needed
to exist in your place

self-sabotaged in my solitary cell
i could sacrifice my ugly smile

i could deprive my senses
and go unseen by my own shadow

sometimes i look back fondly
at feeling nothing

how i reliquished the responsbility
of responding to my pain appropriately

i am not as strong
as i made myself out to be

and not even the pearls of poetry
could pave the potholes in my bones

but i can't hurt myself
without hurting you

and that's what makes love
so frustratingly beautiful

good night aunt madonna
and may mercy make music in your mind

if anyone is owed an easier go
the next time around

it is you
and your gentle heart

it saddens me sincerely
to think about how scarcely you smiled

but even with such a small stature
and a voice that spoke so softly

you still sought to save your sibling
from the one who called him son

and you told yourself you failed
but you did enough

because your brother got to grow up
aware of your secret strength

and knowing that no matter how alone he felt
he was never without his big sister's love

you are a protector
but you still needed protection

and i hope heaven can heal
the wounds that we could not

and all the bugs that once bullied your body
burn up in the atmopshere   . . .

as you ascend to a sanctuary
where your afflictions are forbidden to follow

and where your smile can be seen
from the other side of the sun

so it is in the loveliness of your light
that we look to you in the sky

smile back and sing
good morning aunt madonna

you are the hero of this house
and the habitat of my heart

you found a way to dig up happiness
from what i thought was a hopeless husk

because you have an appetite
for everything except apathy

you are the smile that survived
when i surrendered myself to sadness

and if only you knew
how hearing your steps at the door

helped to heal
all that hurt in my head

you are as much a part of me
as the air sacs in my lungs

or the electricity in my chest
you are the song my ribs protect

you are my every adventure
and all of my favorite things

if i had to wander the whole world
your company would've made it worth it

and if i had found the fountain of youth
i'd have used it to fill your bowl

IT'S OKAY EVERYONE

I'VE KNOWN THIS GENTLE TORMENT

SURE IT IS AN UNWELCOME GUEST

BUT I STILL TREAT IT KIND

LIKE A BUMBLEBEE IN MY SHOE

HOW COULD I CRUSH IT

WHEN FIGHTING AGAINST IT

WOULD ONLY MEAN HURTING MYSELF

you don't have to tell me
how many years it has been

i lost a friend on that day
and have lost him every day since

but if i can still see him
when i close my eyes

and if i can still hear his laugh
in the back of my mind

then why would i say goodbye
and why should i not smile back

there are so many things
i will never understand

today i lost a friend
and i will lose him again tomorrow

love and loss
those two forces are always at odds

but loss only lasts as long as life
whereas love lives on in epilogues

love is a contradiction
like a calamity that calms the countryside

it's a beautiful blizzard of cherry blossoms
that blitzes through my blood

a hurricane in my lungs
that somehow makes it easier to breathe

an earthquake that quietly creaks the floor
a tremor that massages my heart muscle

and if i liken you to a natural disaster my love
it is not because of the destruction that awaits

but because once you make landfall
i will never be the same again

i have this certainty swirling in my head
that the alleys are eavesdropping

and the phantoms who reside there
are foaming at the mouth

smiling sideways with upside down teeth
hissing through obstructed airways

but they aren't that scary
just lonely enough to have never really lived

still they celebrate their small space
despite having been abandoned by all that breathes

remember the alleys are listening
curious as to who treats them like low-lives or leftovers

curious as to who would color them with carnage
they are careful about committing the cruel to memory

but for those who enter the alley
and find friends instead of phantoms

then the scenery begins to shed its city skin
surrendering the skeletons that were sleeping in its cement

and as the alley's anatomy rearranges
there arrives a portal to paradise

i refuse to write a poem
unless i get permission from andromeda

and should that be so
then i give the stars my gratitude

and i start with an idea
of something i once imagined as a kid

like a little girl named pat
which is short for patricide

who wears a jellyfish on her head
and twirls the tentacles when lost in thought

her favorite word is palindrome
but she often uses it in the wrong context

how i would have loved to meet her
and maybe catch garter snakes in her mother's garden

i imagine that she would have enough stories
to entertain an entire galaxy

so that when she grows up
she could happily take my place

you asked me to write you a poem
that could lift your spirits

but instead i wrote
a book about death

and i had the time of my life
breaking your heart

so if i have truly been gifted with words
then surely i have betrayed that blessing

and in my treachery
i became captive to my own creations

but even so
i do not regret these poems

i only ask for forgiveness
for the fact i wrote them in blood

so many people have saved me
in so many subtle ways
and somehow it still slips my mind
to say the simplest thing

Thank you

10% of royalties from this book go towards the National Alliance on Mental Illness (NAMI) in Franklin County, Ohio.

Thank you for your contribution.

About the Author

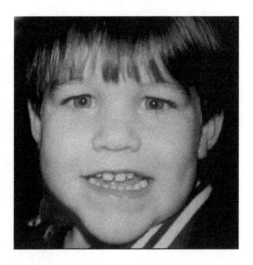

Alec B. Hood is an Ohio native and a distinguished military graduate of Indiana University, in which he double-majored in Creative Writing and Slavic Languages and Literature. Upon graduating, he began his four years of active duty service, completing both the Infantry Officer School and Army Ranger School before being stationed in Fort Drum, New York. After completing his service obligation, Hood switched his focus from the armed services to public safety, returning home to Ohio to work for his home city as a paramedic. Alec married his great love, Margaret, in late 2019, and together, they live with their beloved dogs, Winnie and Otis. Rest in Pretend is Hood's debut poetry collection.

Connect with Alec on Instagram:

@alecthepretendpoet

About the Publisher

INDIE EARTH
PUBLISHING

Indie Earth Publishing is an author-first, independent co-publishing company based in Miami, FL. A publisher for writers founded by a writer, Indie Earth offers the support and technical assistance of traditional publishing to writers without asking them to compromise their creative freedom. Each Indie Earth Author is a part of an inspired and creative community that only keeps growing, making a different one book at a time. For more titles from Indie Earth, or to inquire about publication, please visit:

www.indieearthbooks.com

Instagram: @indieearthbooks

For inquiries, please email:
indieearthbooks@gmail.com

Printed in the USA
CPSIA information can be obtained
at www.ICGtesting.com
LVHW040849140524
780163LV00006B/148